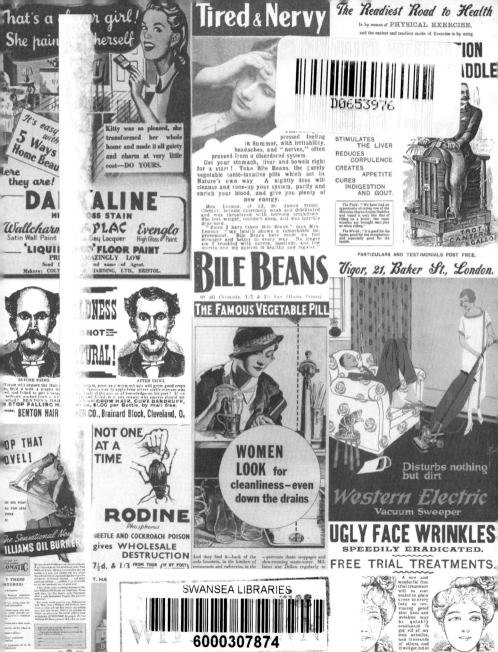

# How To Be An
# ADULT

First published in Great Britain in 2017 by
Michael O'Mara Books Limited
9 Lion Yard
Tremad̶e̶c̶ ̶R̶o̶a̶d̶
Londor̶

A CIP ̶                                              British Library.

ISBN: 978-1-78243-880-9 in hardback print format
ISBN: 978-1-78243-884-7 in e-book format

Front cover illustration by Sam Hadley

Follow us on Twitter @OMaraBooks

www.mombooks.com

Printed and bound in Malta

# How To Be An ADULT

## A Book of Real Help

Michael O'Mara Books Limited

# The Readiest Road to Health

Is by means of PHYSICAL EXERCISE,

and the easiest and readiest mode of Exercise is by using

# VIGOR'S HORSE-ACTION
# —— SADDLE

Which not only provides, as Dr. GEORGE FLEMING, C.C., writes, "**A PERFECT SUBSTITUTE FOR THE LIVE HORSE**" but acts so beneficially upon the system as to be of almost priceless value. It

PROMOTES
    GOOD SPIRITS
QUICKENS THE
    CIRCULATION,
STIMULATES
    THE LIVER
REDUCES
    CORPULENCE
CREATES
    APPETITE
CURES
    INDIGESTION
    AND GOUT.

*The Field*: "We have had an opportunity of trying one of the Hercules Horse-Action Saddles and found it very like that of riding on a horse; the same muscles are brought into play as when riding."

*The World*: "It is good for the figure, good for the complexion, and especially good for the health.

PARTICULARS AND TESTIMONIALS POST FREE.

# INTRODUCTION

This simple little book of Real Help aims to provide some important pointers for all young adults as they set out to fulfil their exciting dreams both in the home and in the world. In it, you'll find tips on all manner of topics – from choosing the right colour distemper for your living room and the right way to budget household expenditure to saying 'Be gone!' to freckles and planning an At Home for important guests. Whether you are a singleton embarking on life's journey or a newly married couple, there is plenty within to ensure you set off along the right path.

However, this is not old, time-worn advice from yesteryear, oh no! There are many innovations to be found, along with ideas to enable you to cut your bills, clean more effectively and make the most of what you have, whether brand spanking new or a mixture of new and hand-me-downs. Remember, as the old saying has it: good furniture alone will not give a room charm (although it is a very important contribution) but colour, arrangement, texture and balance all play their part in producing a harmonious whole. The same could be said of many aspects of life: it is the 'harmonious whole' one aspires to in adult life.

Good luck, young adult!

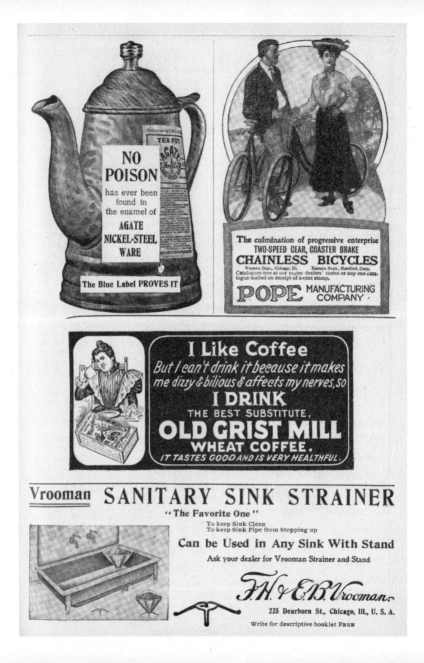

# SELECTING YOUR HOME

Now you're an adult, one of the great joys of life – especially for a married couple – is looking for a new home, a little slice of Paradise to call one's own. Some time ago I came across a charming cottage with a white fence around a lovely garden and roses around the front door, and on passing the little gate I smiled as I read:

"NOW IS THE WINTER OF OUR DISCONTENT MADE GLORIOUS SUMMER" by the use of the

## Incandescent Fire-Mantel

*(PATENTED).*

Makes brilliant, Smokeless Fires, costing in fuel only 2*d.* per day.

**Prices complete, 5s. 6d. to 12s. 6d.**

*NO ALTERATION TO GRATE NECESSARY.*

Obtainable from **2,000 AGENTS** throughout the Kingdom.

### Don't be Easy Prey!

It often happens that a couple are so taken up with themselves that they wander through a house in a maze of bliss and become an easy prey to the blandishments of the agent or landlord. Remember: buying, leasing or renting a house requires careful thought and consideration.

'Dream-Come-True', so apparently its tenants had been lucky enough to find the Ideal Home!

It's all very well for the bride-to-be to indulge in daydreams of the beautiful nest which 'he' and she shall inhabit, but when the time to go house- hunting arrives then they will require all the common sense and practical domestic knowledge they possess to make a happy choice.

## THE POSITION OF WINDOWS

The aspect, to be ideal, should be east and west or south-east. Are the windows a fair size? Are they bright and cheerful, with something of a pleasant outlook?

## POINTS TO CONSIDER

• Remember to ensure that your dream home is affordable. It is incredible to the inexperienced how this, that and the next item mount up in the most unexpected manner and swell the sum total of expenditure.

• Take the locality into account, especially as regards the husband's business; and the cost of his travel has to be added to the overhead charges.

- It is the business of the bride-to-be to indulge in a stern cross-examination about the number of cupboards, the style and size of the windows, the supply or lack of electric lights or gas fittings; the kind of fireplace and cooking stove, the means of obtaining hot water, and the like, remembering that the features of a house which contribute most to its comfort or otherwise are least obvious.

- The seller will not omit to mention all the good points. It's the things he ignores which matter most.

## The Kitchen and Bathroom Premises

The wife or bride must pay particular attention to the kitchen premises, whether she does her own work or employs a maid. Are these convenient to the dining room and the front and back doors? Is the stove in a good light and close to the sink? Is the larder well-ventilated?

Is the bathroom provided with wash-hand basin and geyser and are the sanitary arrangements satisfactory?

## A Garden

Although very delightful, if either husband or wife is prepared to give up time and trouble to it, gardening is one of the happiest and healthiest occupations. However, it also involves expense, and a large one is not usually desirable to the ordinary householder.

## If In Doubt

Where any doubt whatever exists about drainage, soil, construction etc., it is as well to employ a sanitary inspector or an architect to inspect and report. Likewise, it is money well spent to entrust the purchase or leasing to a solicitor, who deals with more details of this kind in a month than the husband is likely to deal with in a lifetime.

# HOME DECORATING

&

Putting one's own mark on the home of one's dreams is always an exciting challenge. However there are certain points one must bear in mind to avoid a miserable mistake!

## COLOUR EFFECTS ON TEMPERS AND NERVES

It has long been known that certain colours affect the nerves of highly sensitive people, making them feel happy, cheerful and comfortable; dignified or frivolous or depressed, if not actually bad tempered, and so on.

Colour also affects the circulation of the blood, and it in turn is responsible for our mental condition and our attitude towards people and things in general.

### Red

- Some employers are placing their typists in red rooms, where they are supposed to work much more energetically than in any other atmosphere.

- On the other hand, red and brilliant shades of orange exert a very bad influence on irritable

---

## STAY AT HOME

Colour experts in America are being kept very busy, advising wives what tint of wallpapers to choose, which will correspond with their husband's aura because, they believe, given the right colour, the men will be perfectly content to stay at home of an evening, instead of going off to their clubs etc.

---

people, who are soothed and refreshed by artistic combinations of violet and green.

## Green

- All spring hues and every shade of green have been proved invigorating.

- Many up-to-date doctors are insisting that the walls of nursing homes and hospitals shall be this colour in the best interests of their patients, who are thus encouraged to make a better fight for health, if not for life, than if surrounded by the cold, monastic severity of a dead white ward.

## Blue

- Reputed not only to have a very calming effect on bad-tempered folks, blue is also the best colour for imparting the appearance of space to a small room. It affords dignity and apparent loftiness, especially when the tints are of the stronger and more intense shades.

### BEWARE!

Pale pink wallpapers never 'go well' with Jacobean oak, although old rose hangings and cushions act as a splendid foil to its sombre colour.

## Tan

- Is the next best colour for imparting the appearance of space in a small room as it absorbs light and gives out a sunny effect.

## Yellow

- Another sunlight colour and even a dark room looks light when papered or distempered in yellow.

## YOUR COLOUR SCHEME

To a great extent this must depend on the aspect of the room, but the first consideration is cheerfulness, the second durability (for no delicate colouring is of use where children are playing about).

A general suggestion would be of warm cream walls, bright cretonne curtains – not too light – and chair covers to match, which would not require to be always in the washtub.

A square of hair carpet or a linoleum-covered floor with a large rug would be ideal for such a homely, cosy room. If one were furnishing such a room at the start of their housekeeping, or when moving into a new home, then as regards furniture, nothing could be more suitable or in better taste than an oak gate-leg table and wheel-back chairs with gaily coloured cushions and, if space permitted, an oak dresser with an array of pretty cottage crockery.

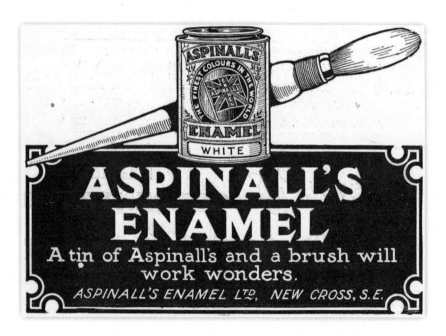

## Distemper or Wallpaper?

The simplest form of distemper is that composed of a whitewash to which the desired colour is added but the trouble with this is that it is very apt to flake and rub off on a passing coat or dress. Water paints or zinc washes are preferable for they do not 'come off' like the former and can be renewed when necessary.

With wallpaper, on the other hand, the choice of papers is an important one and the chief consideration is a bright and cheerful effect. Nothing ensures this better than pretty shades of yellow from the palest primrose to the deepest orange. Pink in most tones lights up well, but blues, mauves, and certain greens and greys are to be avoided as a rule as they tend to be cold-looking.

Paperhanging is an art to itself, but if the walls have been stripped, washed and prepared correctly, the papering of a room is well within the scope of any capable woman, but she would be very well advised to start operations on a small scale, say a tiny bedroom.

### Remember!

Anything patterned has a tendency to make a small room look smaller and a small, finicky design on the walls of a large room looks foolish.

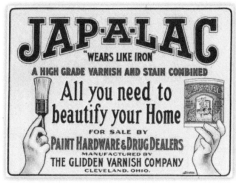

# FURNISHING YOUR HOME

I
t has been well said that an over-furnished house is like an over-dressed woman: never in good taste. Simplicity ought to be the dominating note in any house, large or small, and it need not spell monastic severity, as some are tempted to suppose, but merely the highest expression of utility and beauty. For whatever is purely ornamental is artificial and useless.

Model 398
Regd. Design

## PUT·U·UP
REGD TRADE MARK

### THE WORLD'S BEST VALUE IN DUAL PURPOSE FURNITURE

" Put-u-up " is the supreme settee bed value—only the " Put-u-up " guaranteed mechanism can give the same smooth opening and trouble-free service. The hidden full length bed, with rigid steel framed wire mesh mattress and loose overlay, is as comfortable as an ordinary bed. " Put-u-ups " are made in a wide range of models to match all furnishing schemes. Why not write to the manufacturers (wholesale only) for free literature.
GREAVES & THOMAS LTD., NORTHWOLD ROAD, E.5.

*Certainly!*

SOLD BY ALL GOOD FURNISHERS AND STORES

## THE CHOICE OF FURNITURE

A sense of suitability and the fitness of things must be kept in mind, and it is the height of folly to buy a bargain of a huge piece of furniture which, on account of its size, would look wholly out of place in the average living, dining or drawing room.

It's a matter of personal taste if one furnishes throughout in one wood or colour as regards upholstery. Generally the very best results are obtained by uniformity, leaving the suggestion of richness to be supplied by hangings, carpets, pictures and ornaments.

A few basic 'rules of thumb':

- Furniture should be solid but not stolid, and in simple, artistic outlines of which one never tires.

- Tables should be chosen of the new, expanding order, which can be drawn out to full length in only a moment.

- Chairs should be warranted to stand firm on their feet and not liable to be overturned at the merest touch.

- Armchairs – is the back high enough to rest the head easily? Is the edge of the seat well sprung? If not, within a short time it will likely slant towards the floor and induce considerable discomfort.

- Carpets and rugs should be of a quiet, neutral tint and should harmonize with the walls and not contrast too strongly with any of their surroundings. They must merge with the general scheme of things.

The
**AUTOPHONOLA**
THE SUPER PLAYER PIANO

MAYFAIR STUDIO                    Upright Model 'A'

## THE LIVING ROOM

In many modern homes there is only one apartment other than the bedrooms – namely the living room, which serves as the centre of family life. It should be the largest and sunniest room in the house and it has to cater for all tastes. For example, it may have to accommodate father's big desk and mother's work table, to say nothing of their particular armchairs, a large dining table, perhaps the piano, as well as the children and their toys.

The dining table, from time immemorial has always occupied the centre of the room but there's no reason why it should not be moved close to the window if that it a good size, or to one side near the door where it can more easily be laid out and cleared away when required.

## WHERE THE CHILDREN ARE

The children's needs must be looked after, and if they can have a small table for their lessons and their games, the poor mites will not have to clear away their toys etc., every time a meal is served to the family. This is where a box ottoman, which can also be used as a seat, is most convenient.

The remainder of the furniture should be placed against the walls. If books are among the family's most prized possessions, then they should not be enclosed in bookcases, but in small erections fixed to any odd corner or on a long shelf running right around

It appears very full up already, so there must be the most careful arrangement of furniture and a close economy of space if it is to attain its purpose and a fair amount of comfort and liveableness. Cupboards are essential.

the room and about the height of a dado.

Window seats, if the proper height and cushioned, make very delightful sitting accommodation in the summer. In winter the couch may be wheeled up to within four feet or so of the fire so that everyone can get the benefit of the general heat.

Everyone must, of course, arrange such a room to their own liking, but it is a wise plan to do away with everything which has not a special use, thus avoiding 'dust-traps' and the accumulation of rubbish.

## CURTAINS

Every housewife finds the question of curtains a fascinating one, and loves nothing better than purchasing a new set, for she realises that the appearance of the window hangings, in their dainty, fresh crispness, are the outward and visible index of a comfortable, well-run house, or the reverse.

Some women will keep to the same style and kind of curtains throughout the year and find that casement cloth, fadeless fabrics, Bolton sheeting, etc., are most suitable for this purpose, whilst others vary their drapery according to the season.

Artificial silk materials, with their soft, sheeny effects, are very popular and wear well, and so do

the artificial silk nets which can be had in almost all colours to suit the prevailing schemes of the various rooms. For winter wear, there is nothing handsomer or better fitted to exclude draughts and keep the room cozy than velveteen curtains.

## Choosing a carpet

Whilst it is not of very great importance to the housewife, when she is buying a carpet, to know the details of how it is woven, she should have some idea of the material of

which it is made in order that she may judge its value. A carpet made of wool wears better and keeps its colour better than those of cotton, jute or hemp. However hair is excellent for carpets, though not used as extensively as it deserves. A hair carpet is extremely durable and can therefore be recommended for real hard wear.

# PLANNING THE HOUSEHOLD BUDGET

⟅∿

I f you keep house haphazardly, there's every chance your home will run at a loss. The best way to ensure a successful year is to divide your income for the whole year into tenths.

Once you have allotted your income in this way, take each allotment in turn and apportion as necessary.

It's impossible to lay down any laws about housing, food and operating expenses, for there are so many different points to be taken into consideration, such as whether you have bought or rented your home, the number of meals eaten at home, the size of family, the amount of entertaining, the number of rooms to be lighted or heated and so on.

Equally, it's not easy to make any fixed rules about spending on clothes. How you spend your clothing allowance should depend entirely on your circumstances. If you live in the country you will probably not need it all; if you

---

### DIVIDING YOUR INCOME BOX

Two-tenths — Housing
Five-tenths — Food and Operating Expenses
One-tenth — Clothing
One-tenth — Personal
One-tenth — Health, insurance and savings

---

live in town and have to put in an appearance at numerous social functions, you'll probably find it very difficult to make the allowance come up 'to the scratch'.

Sometimes you may have to 'rob Peter to pay Paul' and cut back on your 'smokes', travel third class when you might prefer to travel first or do without a car.

Whatever you do, remember these key points:

- Rule your home, don't let your home rule you
- Simplify your housekeeping
- Make an art of shopping
- Cook scientifically and not by guesswork

**DROP THAT SHOVEL!**

CAREFREE OIL HEAT IS YOURS FOR LESS THAN EVER BEFORE!

*The Sensational New* **WILLIAMS OIL BURNER**

My experience is that if you don't make a stand at the start of married life about what should be expended on this and what should be expended on that, you'll never be able to straighten out the budget to your mutual satisfaction later on.

## THRIFT IN THE KITCHEN

The housewife who has not acquired the knack of working over into tempting and palatable dishes the odds and ends left from the daily

The most efficient way of shutting off the blues since they first put switches on radios ... *CIGARETTES that really SATISFY!*

**CHESTERFIELD**

*Milder* *better taste*

LIGGETT & MYERS TOBACCO CO

meals has miserably failed in her calling. Wastefulness is extravagance in its worst form, and no place does it assume such gigantic proportions as in the kitchens of the careless or ignorant mistress.

The methodical and truly economical housewife allows nothing, no matter in how small quantities, if eatable, to be thrown away until its possibilities in conjunction with other odds and ends have been reviewed by her. Each morning she takes an

inventory of her larder. Perhaps there will be the remains of a baked or boiled chicken, which, seemingly, is little more than a skeleton, but even in its depleted state this may be made to do duty as the foundation of several appetizing dishes if one but knows how to go about preparing them.

By picking off all the meat which clings to the bones and shredding it, then adding some light biscuit crumbled fine, moistening the whole with the left-over gravy or hot milk and standing in a hot oven for twenty minutes, the result will be a most inviting luncheon dish.

# IN THE KITCHEN

'I couldn't imagine a kitchen now without my patent dresser!' exclaimed a house-proud bride of my acquaintance recently, as we discussed domesticity. We were in her kitchen and she threw open the glass doors of her cabinet and displayed all her stores in spotless and orderly array, pulled out her baking-board and her rolling-pin and showed me how easily and quickly she could make pastry, since flour and everything she required were close at hand.

An indicator with arrows pointing to the sugar and spices etc.,

which were running short, served as a reminder when she went shopping at the end of the week.

## Equipping Your Kitchen

When planning your kitchen, have your equipment grouped in order of use. The work-table should be between the kitchen cabinet and refrigerator and the cooker, and it's a good idea to have the sink opposite the work-table on the other side of the kitchen, with a porcelain-topped collapsible wall-table to take pots and pans after dishing up or to stack dishes on until ready to wash.

Another super kitchen innovation is a two-way cupboard installed between the kitchen and dining room with a serving hatch beneath it – very useful and efficient. However, do beware the clatter of dishes and the smell of cooking coming from the kitchen through the hatch when in use.

## Cooking

The eternal question: gas or electricity? On price, broad comparison tells us that there's not much in it. The advantages of either depend on what sort of person you are and what pleases you best. If you like easy adjustability, not having to plan and think too much and a warm kitchen, you want gas.

### Range Cooking

Nowadays the modern home is equipped with gas or electric cooking facilities, however closed ranges are still *de rigeur* in some households. You may know how to cook on it but are you aware of the proper – and essential – cleaning routine to keep it sparkling? See page 35 for tips on keeping your range in tip-top shape.

**MIRRO**
makes
your pans
gleam
brighter

**KILLS GREASE
IN
10 SECONDS**

If you want perfect cleanliness and smooth working with much careful thought, you want electricity. At least one wants the *possibility* of using electricity, for the sake of the light, the wireless, kettles, toasters and the like.

## Refrigerators

These are worth having in a fairly large family or one which is out to, say, alternate meals, but it is of doubtful advantage for a bachelor woman who takes the joint in and out every day for a week, sometimes letting it hang about for a time before she puts it back. It is, of course, all right if the week's food is cooked on Saturday and each thing never taken out until it is wanted. It is also important never to allow any rancid food to be in the refrigerator ('what *is* it that's smelling so awful around here?') or it will affect the rest of the contents, especially butter, for some time to come, or until the refrigerator is thoroughly washed out.

Until recently it was impossible to own a refrigerator unless you had electricity laid on. Now you have the choice of refrigerators run by electricity, gas and oil, and most models are available in a snow-white enamelled finish as well as in shades to match popular colour schemes.

## SMALL KITCHEN EQUIPMENT

Don't invest in your small kitchen equipment until you've bought and installed all large equipment and can see how much room you have to spare. Here are a few important points to remember when shopping for smaller items.

- Buy the best quality – better to have a few good tools to work with than a quantity of cheap ones.

- Choose sizes or sets of saucepans and frying pans etc., as well as casseroles and pudding basins suitable for normal size of household.

- When you have to choose between a labour-saving gadget and an old-fashioned one, choose the labour saving.

## CUTLERY

It's impossible to give a standard list of cutlery required for kitchen use, but here are a few of the things I find invaluable:

Set of grapefruit knives
1 saw-edged fruit knife
1 palette knife
1 meat knife
Set of vegetable parers
1 boning knife

Set of kitchen carvers
1 saw-edged bread knife
1 chopping knife
1 garnishing knife
1 cook's knife

## SODA: A HOUSEHOLD FRIEND

There are numerous uses to which baking soda can be put, aside from the legitimate ones of cake and bread making.

Try it as a remedy for burns – it really can work wonders. Simply moisten the burned area and apply a thick paste of baking soda, then bandage, reapplying several times until the burning sensation is allayed.

If milk is at souring point, a pinch of soda will restore it to its original sweetness.

A little soda dissolved in warm water will sweeten a sour stomach.

Lamp burners boiled for half an hour in soda and water will cause a lamp to burn with renewed brilliancy.

## PESTS

There is no way in which that household pest, the cockroach, can be banished but by perfect cleanliness in the kitchen and cellar. The first step is to remove all dishes and packages of groceries from the cupboards and shelves as well as all tins that hang from nails in the walls or woodwork. Have ready an ample supply of scalding water and thoroughly scald all the shelves and cracks. Turn the kitchen tables upside down, scald them, remove the shades from the windows and scald the corners thoroughly. Scald not only the possible places but the impossible places as well. Plunge every pot, kettle, dish and pan into a large kettle of boiling water in which you have placed a large handful of washing soda. This will not only cleanse all articles from grease but will kill and remove all tiny eggs that you might overlook.

For the benefit of any stray cockroach that may have escaped, sprinkle borax plentifully around.

# THE HOUSEWIFE'S ALPHABET

## ❧

**A**luminium paint brushed over the black ironwork of a bedroom grate makes a vast improvement in the room, apart from being labour-saving, as it only requires to be dusted.

**B**orax removes tea stains, cleans copper, enamel ware, varnish, paint, windows, and straw hats. Boiled up inside rusty vessels it dispels the rust.

**C**old tea renews mahogany walnut woods. Mixed with tea-leaves and poured into stained water carafes, it quickly removes all traces of brown.

Decanters need never become stained if they are rinsed thoroughly with cold water immediately after they are emptied. Half fill the bottle with warm water, add a teaspoonful each of salt and vinegar and a handful of washed tea-leaves. Allow this mixture to remain in the decanter for two to three hours, shaking occasionally during that time. Rinse in cold water. Dry the outside with a soft cloth, polish with a chamois leather, and place neck downwards in a jug to drain.

Enamel saucepans which have a small hole in the bottom can still be used. Pour some dry flour over the hole, then pour in a little boiling water and it will be found possible to cook in the saucepan without the contents leaking at all.

Fruit stains on white materials may be removed by pouring boiling water over them, or if of long standing, applying a weak solution of oxalic acid.

Glassware is difficult to keep bright. The best method of washing glass is to use warm, soapy water, softened by a little powdered borax. Rinse the articles in clean, cold water, turn them upside down on a tray to drain before drying them well with a linen glass-cloth. Finish with a rub of a chamois leather.

Hair-brushes which have become soft can be made quite hard and firm by dipping them into a strong solution of alum. Put a little alum in some hot water. A pennyworth of alum will last for months.

If you want real comfort on a hot summer day, fill the hot water bag with cold water, and put it under your cheek during the afternoon nap.

Just a rub of furniture polish to all brasses after they have been polished will keep them bright longer.

Keep your little kitchen table clean and white by mixing the following ingredients: some dissolved soap, half a pound of sand, and half a pound of lime. Put the mixture on with a scrubbing

brush, and wash off with plenty of cold water.

Leathers: soak in soapy water to which has been added three tablespoonfuls of household ammonia. Move about and press out the dirt. Rinse well in tepid water. Dry in the shade, and pull frequently to keep them soft and pliable.

Medicine bottles may be rid of strong smells by powdering black mustard seeds, adding some warm water, and leaving for a short time. Shake the mixture well.

Nails which have rusted in holes may be loosened by dropping paraffin or kerosene over them and letting it soak in.

Olive oil restores the polish to tables that have been marked by hot dishes if the marks are first painted with spirit of nitre. Boiled linseed oil renovates leathers and also brightens paints and varnish.

Pewter that is very dirty can be cleaned by soaking it for three or four days in water with a small quantity of potash added. Then it should be rubbed with a clean duster dipped in olive oil mixed with precipitated chalk. Polish with a dry, soft duster.

Quite the best way of keping silver spoons and forks bright is by washing them in warm, soapy water to which has been added a teaspoonful of borax. Dry and polish with leather.

Remove most stains by using lemon juice.

Stained knives may be easily cleaned by sprinkling a little bicarbonate of soda with bath-brick or emery.

Tiles on hearth may be repainted to match any colour scheme by stirring the white of one egg into the paint used. This gives a splendid effect and makes them like new.

# HOUSEHOLD CLEANING

❧

## THE RANGE

It is one of life's muckier jobs but it has to be done! So roll up your sleeves and let's use some elbow grease! When about to clean a range, close the kitchen door and windows to prevent the dust from blowing about.

Every day (if the range has been in use):
- Cinders raked out into cinder box
- All ash brushed away from every part
- Polish range with brush (no need to black lead it every day)
- Rub all steel parts over with a cloth or emery paper
- Empty ash-pan or cinder-box
- Remove all dust from the hearth, wash and whiten
- Clean fender with fire irons
- Once a week the following extra cleaning should be carried out:
- Open dampers and clear flues of soot
- Remove rings from top of range and free from soot
- Remove the little door or slide underneath the oven and rake out soot

---

### MIRRORS

Never use water on a mirror; it might seep down the back of the mirror and produce a mould, which will utterly destroy the silvering and, in time, ruin the glass. All that's needed is a clean rag dipped in either methylated spirits or paraffin and polish with a leather or old newspaper.

---

- Brush out oven and then wipe out with cloth rung out in hot soda water
- Remove any grease that may have been spilt on the range
- Blacklead range and polish

And you're finished! But do remember to have the range chimney swept every six months.

## Cleaning the Windows

Choose a dull day for cleaning the windows but make sure you leave them alone in frosty weather.

Take a painter's brush and dust the windows inside and out before washing them with warm water and vinegar – on no account use soap. Use a small duster wrapped round a pointed stick to clean out all the corners and crevices and wipe dry with a cotton duster (no linen, it leaves threads behind). Polish with old newspaper and you'll soon have a thrilling shine!

## Doorsteps

To keep your doorstep free from ice simply add a cupful of methylated spirits to the pail when you wash your step.

## Draughty Doors

When doors do not close properly, but leave cracks through which draughts enter, place a strip of putty along the jambs, cover the edge with chalk, and shut it. The putty will then fill up all the spaces. Chalk rubbed on the edges prevents adhesion. The putty is left in places where it soon dries and leaves a perfectly fitting jamb.

## A Remedy for Flies

There is nothing more unsightly or obnoxious than the old-fashioned fly-papers, and these are not at all necessary if a pot of mignonette is

kept in any room infested by these pests. Another effective remedy is to drop a little pennyroyal on sheets of blotting paper and place them on the shelves of larder or cupboard.

## Laundry

Should laundry have to be done in the home, have the wash copper placed near the sink and, if possible, let one corner of the kitchen be given up to a corner cupboard in which a collapsible ironing table is permanently fixed. Have a shelf at the top to take electric irons – and have a plug wired in to use when ironing.

A small sink is a nuisance – especially on washday! The ideal arrangement is a double sink – usually metal – and plenty of room for wringing out laundry from the wash copper.

The real problem of washing at home, however, is the drying. One new innovation is the drying cabinet. They are still developing towards maximum efficiency, but what a difference they can make to those endless days of clothes drying around the house!

## MARKING OF LINEN

Linen should be marked with good quality marking-ink, and a special pen provided with the ink should be used so as to obviate damage to the material. Hand-embroidered monograms and initials always enhance the attractiveness of good linen.

Personal taste can of course be exercised in the marking of linen, but each piece should be fully marked with the owner's name, the year purchased, number in the set and the number of the particular article. The following is an example:

### F. H. BURNINGHAM
### 5    1936    12

This indicates that the husband's first Christian name begins with an 'F' and the wife's with an 'H'; '12' indicates that the set, whether of sheets, table-napkins, tea-towels or pillow-cases, consists of 12 articles, and that this particular article happens to be No. '5'.

# MAKING FURNITURE
## AS GOOD AS NEW

When one is setting up home for the first time it is not always possible to have everything brand spanking new and there really is so much that can be done with older pieces to brighten them up and give them a new lease of life!

## UPHOLSTERY

If a vacuum cleaner is available it is no trouble to keep upholstered couches and chairs in good order; but if they have to be cleaned by hand, then they should be removed outside, if possible, and thoroughly beaten with a cane, special attention being paid to the corners in search for traces of moths, etc., which may be eradicated by pressing with a hot iron on brown paper.

## TAPESTRY COVERS

If not very soiled, tapestry covers may be cleaned with a piece of stale bread, or sponged all over with petrol, care being exercised that no fire or light is anywhere near. Another plan is to apply a mix of bran and petrol, leave for an hour or

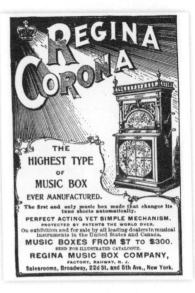

so, and then brush off with a clean, stiff whisk.

## LEATHER COVERED CHAIRS

The lustre of morocco chairs may be restored by simply applying the white of an egg with a sponge and polishing with a soft, clean duster. If, however, they are very shabby, they require more attention with a solution of rye flour and boiling water, brushed lightly on, followed by a varnish of bleached shellac,

### A WICKER CHAIR THAT SAGS?

Sagging may be prevented by rubbing the chair with warm salt and washing with hot water and melted borax, which also prevents discolouration. Dry in the open air. If rather shabby, a pretty cushion of jaupe cotton chintz or floral cretonne will quite disguise its shortcomnigs.

methylated spirit and the white of an egg. Sponge this all over and rub with a chamois leather. Hey presto – a splendid gloss finish!

## Little Tricks

**Stained furniture** – revive and clean by washing with a little methylated spirit dropped into a small quantity of lukewarm water. White stains left by hot items – these will sometimes disappear by simply holding a hot plate over them and then polishing. If this is not effectual, rub in a little olive oil and pour a few drops of spirits of salt or camphor on the spot, rubbing dry with a duster.

**Woodworms** – these little blighters can cause incalculable mischief in old furniture and tend to spread to other items if left untreated. The most effective treatment, once a fortnight, is a bath of paraffin in

which a block of camphor has been dissolved. Squirt into the holes with an old scent spray.

**Scratches on Furniture** – wash the piece with clean, cold water and remove the polish with a rag dipped in paraffin. Take a warm iron and pass it smartly over the area, and in doing so the steam arising will bring the scratch to the surface level. If necessary, smooth with a fine glasspaper sprinkled

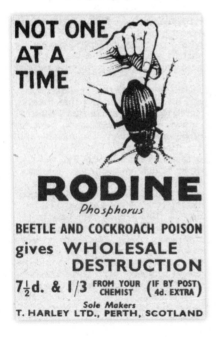

## PAINTED FURNITURE

Painted furniture is having a vogue at present and it is quite within the scope of the amateur to transform a shabby old piece of furniture into a thing of beauty.

The first coat of paint is not usually very satisfactory in appearance, but the second coat requires careful, upright strokes – first up and down, then across and across – so as to ensure smoothness.

with linseed oil and then apply a preparation of beeswax, turpentine and resin and your table or chest of drawers will look like new.

**Old oak** – a little linseed rubbed into the wood two or three times a year should be sufficient to keep oak in good order.

## Rag Rugs from Old Stockings

Mats can easily be made from old woollen stockings. The legs are cut down from top of leg to heel in 1-inch strips. These strips are then unravelled, leaving three or four stitches at one edge to sew by. The strips are sewn on by this edge to a piece of sacking, cut to your preferred size, beginning at the outside and making every row of wool overlap the previous one. The wool may be cut in equal length and drawn with a crochet hook through thick canvas. Old fringes from curtains etc., may be utilized for the same purpose.

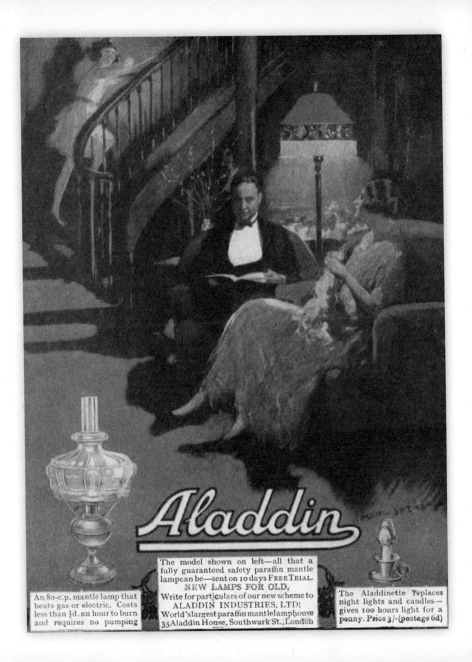

# Aladdin

# LIGHTING YOUR HOME

The question of how a house is to be lighted is an important one, and in most cases may be left to an expert, although it is well that the tenant or owner should express some preference in the matter and arrange that the lights be placed where most desired and not too high.

Matters to consider:

- Electric lights are usually placed in the centre of the room but often so high up and in such opaque bowls that the light is expended chiefly on the ceiling instead of on the lower parts.

**"FAIRY" LIGHT.**
With Double Wicks, in Boxes containing 6 Lights and Glass, burn 10 hours each.

1s. per box.

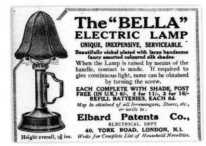
- Add to the brightness of the fireside by placing a light either side or, failing that, a reading lamp on a small table is a great comfort for reading or needlework.

- Shades are easily bought these days and they take all sorts of shapes and sizes, some are veritable works of art. But there's nothing to beat a pretty silk shade with or without the finish of fringes or tassels. Note, though, that as a rule the one colour to be avoided is blue.

- The present fashion is largely for parchment, embellished with quaint scenes or Japanese figures.

## INEXPENSIVE DECORATIVE LIGHTING

Almost any jar can be converted into a lamp, particularly ones that have had a lid. The lid of a syrup or other air-tight tin is required, fitting as well as possible. Get a standard lamp holder that has a screw-nipple, make a hole in the lid fitting the nipple, wind it in and tighten it up on the other side with a nut or a stiff, rubber washer, forced on and glued. Make another hole for the flex to come out at and – hey presto! – you have a very adequate lamp fitting, ready for the lampshade of your choice.

# KEEPING YOUNG
# AND BEAUTIFUL

~

## CARE OF THE COMPLEXION

If the skin is uncomfortably harsh, rub it with an emollient after each ablution. Glycerine and rose-water mixed will also generally be found beneficial, but if Glycerine is unsuitable, virginal milk or pure elderflower water can be used to bathe the face with impunity.

Abjure the use of carmine, rouges, white-lead and the like. The finest cosmetic is rainwater. Soap is very good. Of course there are soaps and soaps: some highly coloured and objectionable, others pure and good. White-lard unscented soap is best.

Food influences the complexion very much. Water drinkers, as a rule, have complexions of greater purity than those who take wine or beer. The cooler the diet the better. Take fruit, vegetables and milk in abundance, but condiments and French sauces have nothing to recommend them.

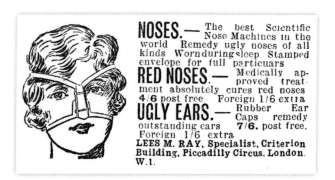

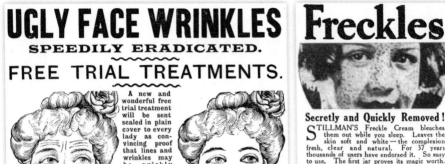

### Wrinkles and Freckles

Often described as 'furrows caused by the skin becoming too loose and large for the organs it has to cover', melancholy and lymphatic constitutions are those which wrinkle soonest. On the face, if the lines are produced by frowning, the remedy is in our own hands. Wrinkles and 'crows feet', if taken in an early stage, may receive a check, but after a certain point all efforts are useless.

When the skin is stimulated into vigorous action by the heat of the summer sun, the result often appears in the form of 'freckles' or 'liver spots', which fade away as the autumn advances. Their departure can be hastened by the frequent application of buttermilk or a mixture of equal parts of lime-water and elderflower water. (For freckles and sunburn the old-fashioned cure of washing with milk is not to be despised.)

## Hands

Roughness of skin is sometimes constitutional but is more generally the result of carelessness in failing to dry the hands properly.

❧

To produce soft white hands there is no necessity to sleep in gloves smeared with grease: the custom is an offensive one. But glove-wearing in the daytime, when one is engaged in any kind of work that is likely to soil the skin, is earnestly to be commended.

❧

For swollen hands, apply a little glycerine and rose-water lotion, wiping off the superfluous moisture with a soft rag.

❧

For chapped hands, there's nothing better than purified lard, spermaceti or an oil of any kind.

## The Figure

### Obesity

Sometimes obesity is constitutional and neither exercise nor rigid diet will reduce it to any great extent. But very often it is due to inactivity, rich living, or an over-abundance of food, even though plain. In the latter cases the remedy is obviously sufficient exercise and simple diet in small quantities. Violent measures suddenly resorted to with a view to reducing flesh will injure the health.

As regards food, abstain from anything of a fatty nature and strike out from the menu potatoes, sugar, milk and butter (except in very small quantities), new bread, stout, rice, cocoa and suet. Take such things as lean meat, toast or dry biscuits, lemon juice and water, weak tea, stewed fruit, vegetables in small quantities and light wine, if fancied, for dinner or luncheon.

## Leanness

Many slim women are distressed by over-prominent bones in the neck and the hollowing of the neighbouring skin, causing what are known as 'salt-cellars'. The only remedy is to try to encourage general plumpness, paying special attention to massage at this portion of the body.

Vocal exercises and bodily gymnastics are also useful. In the case of thin arms use dumb-bells regularly three times a day. It will be strange if in a very short while the muscles are not developed and the arms made far more shapely.

## THE HAIR

The popular notion that each strand of hair is a tube is erroneous. Human hairs are solid. A healthy head needs little more than washing, brushing and combing. If the hair is regularly brushed twice a day, it will be much less likely to require oils and tonics, its growth will be stimulated in the most desirable way and an accumulation of dandruff will be prevented.

Generally speaking, the head should be shampooed once in three to four weeks, in winter during fogs more frequently. After shampooing, dry with a soft towel and rub the scalp until it glows.

One of the finest treatments for the hair is to let it flow loosely, allowing the air to penetrate, and rub the scalp gently but firmly with the tips of the fingers. This simple but healthy plan will, if followed, greatly improve the hair and stimulate young growth.

It is generally advisable to cut the tips of the hair about once in four to six weeks. The plan of keeping the hair closely cropped for a few years rarely fails to produce luxuriant growth.

The use of curling irons has a deleterious effect upon the hair, making it unnaturally dry and hot. Simple waving pins are therefore to be preferred.

**Mrs. S. A. Allen's**
World's
**Hair Restorer.**

Never
Fails.

Quickly changes
gray hair to its
natural
colour.

It is not an
experiment but
has been in use
for over sixty
years throughout
the civilised
world. It is the
best, and the
best is always
the cheapest.

Cut this adv. out and send it, together with
P.O.O. or stamps **4s.,** to 114, Southampton
Row, London, and a FULL-SIZED LARGE
BOTTLE will be sent CARRIAGE PAID
anywhere in the United Kingdom.     H

"YOUR HAIR IS
SIMPLY LOVELY
TONIGHT – I FEEL
TERRIBLY
ROMANTIC"

"THANKS TO
CAMILATONE GOLDEN RINSE
– BUT THAT'S MY SECRET

*Camilatone*
**Golden
Rinse**
2 D
PER PACKET
FROM HAIRDRESSERS
& CHEMISTS EVERYWHERE

### NATURAL CURLS

There is a theory that naturally curling hair can be
encouraged by brushing the hair upwards or backwards
when it first appears at any length on a child's head.

# MANNERS MAKETH MAN ...
# WOMAN AND CHILD!

Frequent breaches of good manners are found in noisy laughter, exaggerated gesturing, loud talking and the vulgar discussion of the speaker's private affairs – or those of others – in tones which may be heard by everyone travelling in the same bus or train.

Amongst those guilty of breaches of etiquette in public, we find:

- Persons of both sexes who walk several abreast along the pavement so that other pedestrians are forced into the road.

- Persons of both sexes who hustle unfairly to get on crowded public vehicles or push into them arrogantly while others are alighting.

the finishing touch to a lovely make-up

**SWANDOWN**
*Lipstick*

IN 7 EXCITING SHADES

LIGHT · MEDIUM · DARK CYCLAMEN
ROSE PINK · ROSE CERISE · CHERRY · FLAME

LIPSTICK RE-FILLS AVAILABLE

Nearly every woman finds
She's prettier still by using " Hinde's."

Hinde's, Ltd., Patentees and Manufacturers of Brushes and Toilet Articles,
BIRMINGHAM AND LONDON.

* People who will talk during concert, theatre and broadcasting performances, and those who at the cinema persist in reading sub-titles aloud or disclose the unfolding of the plot before it is shown on the screen, and those who use too much perfume, fidget or cough unnecessarily, or smoke in such a careless manner as to cause discomfort to their neighbours.

## GENTLEMEN FRIENDS

When any gentleman, newly introduced to a girl, has escorted her home from the scene of the introduction, it is not correct for her to ask him to call, or for him to seek the permission from her. Any such invitation must come from the girl's mother, or any friends with whom she is staying, so if she wishes to see more of her cavalier, she should introduce him to her mother or hostess.

When living in a boarding house, it may be impossible for her to entertain a man friend there at all; perhaps she may not even ask him to call for her, or at best they can only be together under the curious gaze of other residents.

The same difficulty besets the girl who has made a little bachelor 'nest' for herself. She cannot ask a gentleman for tea or a pleasant evening out without bowing to convention, at least to the extent of securing the presence of a girl friend as well. She must tread warily if she values her own good name.

# HAVING PEOPLE IN

The success of an informal 'At Home' usually stands or falls by the ability of the hostess to keep her guests circulating. When all have arrived, she should go from group to group and see that old friends have the opportunity to talk to each other, or introduce people of similar tastes, never staying too long with one group.

A smart afternoon dress and no hat is worn by the hostess. If friends are helping you, they should wear their hats, unless actually staying in the house.

For the newly marrieds' 'At Home' the hour of your first 'At Home' must, of course, be arranged to suit your husband and his friends.

In the case of small, afternoon At Homes, quite simple refreshments suffice, such as tea, coffee, lemonade – possibly claret cup – thin bread and butter, a sufficient variety of cakes, all of which should be of a suitably negotiable nature, and tiny savoury cress or cucumber sandwiches are always popular. Hot buttered toast and teacakes are delicious in wintertime but these should be served with due regard for their embarrassingly greasy nature.

ORIGINAL AND BECOMING

**TEAFROCK**

FOR PRESENT WEAR

" ENA "

**Attractive Tea Dance Frock,** made in the new Irene Lace mounted over crêpe de Chine to tone, long sleeved bodice, new circular fronted skirt and straight back, trimmed self crêpe de Chine. In Mushroom, Nigger, Sand, Ecru, Black.

*Special Price*

**£5 . 19 . 6**

Outsize **21/-** extra.

Theatre Ticket Bureau
on the Lower Ground Floor,
Now Open.

**MARSHALL &
SNELGROVE**
VERE-STREET-AND-OXFORD-STREET
LONDON·W.1

# Conversation

The art of conversation is to know how to listen. All other gifts are, as it were, the icing on the cake. If you really wish to please in conversation, learn to make others talk; study your friends' tastes, and take a genuine interest in them. Don't be afraid to ask for an explanation if something becomes too technical. This is flattering to the speaker and wise from your point of view, since it may save you from some foolish remark caused by a misunderstanding. But beware of the childish or 'helpless woman' pose, which can be irritating.

Subjects of an unpleasant nature should be kept out of the conversation. Private worries, family jars and distressing details concerning accident or illness are also among the subjects not fit for social conversation. Sarcasm, that cheap form of wit which gets a laugh at the expense of others, and the telling of risqué stories are alike signs of ill-breeding.

## Verbal Introductions

*Introduce:*

*1. A gentleman to a lady, whatever their respective ranks;*

*2. A lady or gentleman of lower rank to one of higher rank;*

*3. An unmarried lady to a married, unless the former is of higher rank;*

*4. A younger lady or gentleman to an elder if of equal rank.*

The person being introduced is always named first, the correct form being 'May I introduce Mr. A. to Miss B.'

On introduction, both should say 'How do you do?' but not shake hands unless the person of higher rank or the elder offers her hand as a sign of favour.

## BRIDGE

One of the most delightful ways of entertaining is to give a bridge party, afternoon or evening, just as you please. If you decide on bridge with refreshments only, tea for the afternoon and coffee and sandwiches for the evening, send out 'At Home' cards with 'Bridge' and the time written in the lower left-hand corner. If the game is held without lunch or dinner as a prelude, you can serve coffee before starting to play, and accompany it with liqueurs if you please. Have the coffee ready fifteen minutes before you wish to play, and offer it with crème de menthe, crème de cacao, or any of the other liqueurs that women generally prefer to cognac. Cognac must, however, be in evidence if men are of the party.

It is now the fashion to ask guests to remove their hats before sitting down to bridge, no matter when it is played, but the up-to-date hostess does not feel it necessary to have them shown to a bedroom to do this, if she can provide an impoverished dressing-table below a mirror near the card-room. She

provides there a selection of face powders for all complexions, a jar of cotton wool tufts, a container for the soiled wool, a clothes brush, and a pin cushion so that any necessary titivating can be done before the guest is announced.

## EMERGENCY ENTERTAINING

Some hostesses make no end of a fuss when the Man of the House brings a friend home unexpectedly for supper. Now there's something very wrong if a hostess cannot provide a meal at any and every time. It is a slur on her powers as a caterer. Have a well-stocked emergency shelf in your larder and near it suspend a tin-opener, contrivances for opening sardine tins, cider, lemonade bottles and the like. The shelf itself should contains items such as: olives (plain and stuffed), pickles (sweet and sour), gherkins, tomato catsup, small bottles of mushroom and Worcestershire sauce, all the vinegars, olive oil, mayonnaise, a selection of tinned and bottled soups, vegetables, meat extracts, fish and meat packed in tins and fish and meat pastes in glass pots. Tinned fruits, jams, marmalades, fruit syrups for drinks, condensed milk, evaporated cream and milk, marshmallow cream, cocoa, coffee, tins of cheese biscuits and sweet biscuits, a bottle of grated Parmesan and a tin of cheese fingers.

Remember: whatever you take

for use from this shelf must be replaced at once from your next grocery order.

## A PLEASANT WAY TO ENTERTAIN IN HOT WEATHER

Social obligations don't stop just because it's hot, and as a means of discharging these obligations, the breakfast party, which is relatively newly in vogue, grows in popularity. The reason is obvious: the hour and attendant informality rob the function of many irksome conventionalities which an evening affair imposes upon a hostess – and when the thermometer is hovering at uncomfortable levels, this is no small consideration.

However, just because breakfast is less formal, certain rules do still apply, and the canny hostess does not invite criticism and flaunt her ignorance by disregarding these rules.

Firstly, the invitation must be written in the first person; the hour must not be later than twelve-thirty; if in the country,

sweet course which includes coffee. Formerly, ices in any shape were not in good form for breakfast; now, however, especially if the hour is late, the custom is sanctioned.

## IDEAS FOR THE PERFECT BREAKFAST MENU

- Grapefruit – the ideal breakfast fruit. Serve it halved, sprinkled liberally with sugar and half a Maraschino cherry in its centre. Delightful.

- Shirred eggs in paper cases – why not make the paper cases at home?

- Fish cutlets with cream sauce or fried cod balls

- Asparagus pâté

- Fried spring chicken with hot rolls or creamed chicken

- Cottage cheese salad in tomato cups

where people as a rule rise early, ten-thirty will be better; the table appointments and decorations must have simplicity for their keynote, though elegance is, as ever, our watchword! The menu, though appetizing, must comprise only a few daintily prepared dishes, and the service must be unobtrusive.

The etiquette of breakfast demands that the meal begin with fruit in some form, then shall follow in due order an egg course, fish, an entrée, one meat, a salad and a

- Ice cream frozen in a canteloupe mold, served with dainty wafers

- Coffee

Even an amateur should find it easy to cook and serve such a breakfast!

## WHEN ENTERTAINING GIRLFRIENDS

There are times, perhaps when welcoming a newcomer to the locality or inviting acquaintances who might – just might! – become friends, when a tea party or light supper is called for. I attended one such recently and, when supper was finished, we all repaired to the sitting room and held a 'housekeeping contest'. Each of us was given a piece of paper and a pencil and told to write twelve practical suggestions about housekeeping – one way to make the house prettier, one way to lessen labour, keep the kitchen work smooth, varying menus, decorating the dining table etc., and we were told to end our papers

with an original definition of the meaning of the ideal housekeeper. These papers were then read and discussed and votes taken as to the best and a prize awarded. This housekeeping party was such a great success that it was the beginning of a domestic club which met many times after that.

## THE NEW BRIDE AT HOME

Upon coming to her new home, a bride moving in formal circles usually gives several At Homes in quick succession, sending out afternoon or evening At Home cards, each mentioning the various dates, to friends and relations who attended the wedding or sent presents.

If not moving in circles where the formal routine of calling and card-leaving is observed, she should still give some little 'afternoons' or 'housewarmings' to friends and relations of her own and her husband's, especially those who have sent presents, or neighbours who have already approached them in a friendly spirit. This is, of course, providing that the latter are people whose acquaintance she and her husband wish to cultivate.